To the Limit

Ian Rohr

D1496000

sundance™

A Haights Cross Communications ✦® Company

Copyright © 2003 Sundance/Newbridge Educational Publishing, LLC

This edition of The Real Deal is published
by arrangement with Blake Education.
All rights reserved. No part of this publication
may be reproduced or transmitted in any form
or by any means, electronic or mechanical,
including photocopy, recording, or any
information or retrieval system, without
permission in writing from the publisher.

Published by
Sundance Publishing
P.O. Box 740
One Beeman Road
Northborough, MA 01532–0740
800-343-8204
www.sundancepub.com

Copyright © text Ian Rohr
Copyright © illustrations Cliff Watt

First published 2002 by
Blake Education, Locked Bag 2022, Glebe 2037, Australia
Exclusive United States Distribution: Sundance Publishing

Design by Cliff Watt in association with
Sundance Publishing

To the Limit
ISBN-13: 978-0-7608-6688-7
ISBN-10: 0-7608-6688-0

Photo Credits:
pp. 9, 14, 15 (left), 28–29: Australian Picture Library

Printed in China

Table
of Contents

Extreme Speed

You're on a roller coaster, speeding up and around the curves. You've left your stomach at the last turn.

Going fast can be frightening and fun—like hurtling downhill on a bike or a skateboard. You think you'll make the corner at the bottom, but are you going too fast? People do all sorts of things to get up speed. They race cars, hurtle down mountains on skis and sleds, and skim along the streets on skateboards.

Speed Thrills

Q: When do you go as fast as a racing car?
A: *When you're in it.*

Many of us seem to have a need for speed. Circus rides, skateboards, and action movies give us a "buzzy" feeling caused by an **adrenaline** rush. Our heart beats faster and all of our senses are on alert. We feel we are "on the edge."

Adrenaline is a **hormone** that gets the body ready for action. In extreme sports, this is very important. To take part in these supercharged events, the body needs to be prepared and strong enough to tackle heights, speed, and danger. When our brain senses stress, it tells the adrenal glands to release adrenaline into our blood. This speeds up everything in our body. Our heart pumps faster, sending more oxygen to our muscles. Soon, we're ready for anything!

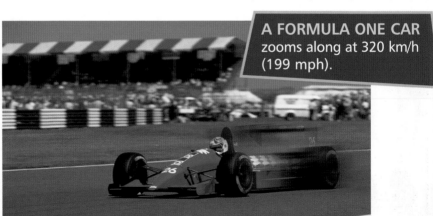

A FORMULA ONE CAR zooms along at 320 km/h (199 mph).

JET FIGHTERS streak through the sky at 3,218 km/h (1,999 mph).

FASTEST	VEHICLE/PLACE	YEAR	SPEED REACHED
WATER			
Jet-speed boat	*Spirit of Australia*	1978	511 km/h (317 mph)
Waterskiing	Australia	1983	230 km/h (143 mph)
Sailing vessel	*Yellow Pages Endeavour*	1993	85.5 km/h (53 mph)
AIR			
Military aircraft	Lockheed SR-71A	1976	Av. 3,530 km/h (2,193 mph)
Passenger jet	Concorde	1976: first flight	2,124 km/h (1,320 mph)
LAND			
Train	Bullet train/Japan	1964: built	261 km/h (162 mph)
Skateboard	US	1998	100 km/h (62 mph)
Production car	McLaren F1	1998	386 km/h (240 mph)
Snowboarding	France	1999	201 km/h (125 mph)
Roller coaster	Steel Dragon/Japan	2000: opened	149 km/h (93 mph)

Road Racers

You're speeding down a road, flat on your back on a special skateboard. You have no brakes and you're only a few inches above the ground. That's street luge. It is based on a winter sport in which people on sleds hurtle down winding icy courses at amazing speeds.

Street luge is one of the fastest sports that doesn't involve an engine. Lugers steer their speeding sleds by shifting their weight slightly to the right or left. They lift their heads just a little to see where they are going.

Anyone who's ridden a bicycle or a skateboard too fast knows about hitting the ground. At 110 kilometers per hour (68 mph), the gravel-rash can be deadly. Lugers have to wear full-face helmets and tough, streamlined clothing.

Clocking on!

There are three types of street luge races. In dual races, two street lugers race against each other. In mass races, four to eight lugers battle it out on the course. In timed races, one luger tries to beat the clock. A luger in California was clocked at just over 135 km/h (84 mph)!

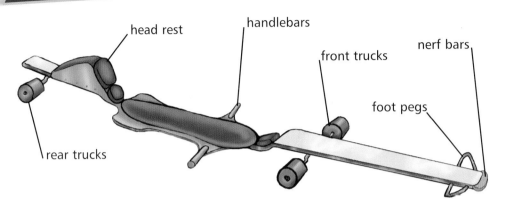

head rest

handlebars

front trucks

nerf bars

foot pegs

rear trucks

LUGERS stop by dragging their feet along the road.

It's All Downhill

Would you plunge down the side of a mountain on skis? Speed skiers do—at speeds of 240 kilometers per hour (149 mph). This takes cool nerves and a lot of skill.

STEEP SLOPES like these are found in only a few places in the world.

Rocks, boulders, and trees can be deadly, so helmets are essential. **Avalanches** can also be a danger, so you need to carry a special light. Then you can be found and dug out of the snow if you are buried by an avalanche.

In 1999, skier Harry Egger of Austria set off down a mountain in France. By the time he reached the bottom, Harry had set a new world record of 248 kilometers per hour (154 mph). When he got to the bottom of the mountain, he vomited.

SPEED SKIING is dangerous. Crevasses can open up without warning, and bad weather can close in quickly.

Extreme Adventure

Would you jump from a skyscraper with a rope around your ankle? Would you crawl deep inside the planet or surf in the sky?

At times, adventure finds you. But sometimes, you go looking for it. You seek adventure in books, on movie screens, and in computer games. Whatever makes your heart beat faster, it's waiting out there! Adventures are exciting, but they can be very dangerous. You need to keep your head and know all the risks before you begin.

Hanging by a Thread

Imagine diving from a four-story-high platform. Vines around your ankles are all you have to keep you from slamming into the ground. You'd choose your vines well and measure their lengths carefully. The idea is to come close to the ground—not hit it!

The vine divers of Vanuatu in the South Pacific were the original bungee jumpers. Today's bungee jumpers tie ropes, not vines, around their ankles. The first bungee jump was an April Fool's Day prank when four friends leapt from a bridge in England.

WITH VINES tied to their ankles, boys in Vanuatu jump from a 25-meter (82-ft.) tower.

New Zealander A. J. Hackett bungeed 324 meters (1,062 ft.) from the Eiffel Tower in 1987. He opened the world's first commercial jump site in New Zealand the following year. Many people free-fall about 50 meters (164 ft.) there for a thrill they don't forget quickly!

THE EIFFEL TOWER in Paris, France

A BUNGEE JUMPER leaps from a hot air balloon.

All BASEs Covered

If you jumped off your front step, a low bridge, or a big boulder, you wouldn't be a BASE jumper. If you jumped from the Leaning Tower of Pisa (56 meters/183 ft.) with a parachute, you'd be on the way to becoming one. You might be arrested though, because BASE jumping is usually illegal.

The "birdman" demonstrates the lost art of head gliding.

The name BASE comes from the four jumping-off points.

Buildings   **A**ntennas   **S**pans   **E**arth

Like a sky diver, you drop with a parachute to stop you, but things move quickly in a BASE jump. You have to balance the thrill of the fall with opening the parachute in time to land in one unbroken piece.

A BASE JUMPER FREE-FALLS from a building and then releases a pilot chute that opens the main parachute.

Deep, Dark Depths

Caving, also called **spelunking,** takes us deep within the earth. Down in the dark, it is a very different world. Flickering flashlights guide the way, and dripping water is the only sound.

Q: What did the caveman have for lunch?

A: A club sandwich.

Caving involves a lot of crawling, squeezing, sliding, and stooping—often in mud and water. It is not for people who are **claustrophobic** (dislike being in tight spaces) or those who want to keep their clothes clean. But caving offers amazing sights: gigantic chambers and deep black holes, underground lakes and rivers, and beautiful formations called **stalagmites** and **stalactites**. Perhaps best of all, though, caving often means exploring a place where no one else has been before.

Cavers just have to be sure they can find their way back up— and out!

HELMETS protect cavers from falling rocks and low ceilings.

Those hard hats are driving me batty!

Stalactites hang from the roof of a cave.

Stalagmites rise up from the floor of the cave.

Surfing the Airwaves

Does standing on a surfboard 10,668 meters (35,000 ft.) up in the air strike fear in your heart? Not if you're into skysurfing. It was developed in the 1980s by skydivers who were bored with their range of twists and turns. They wanted to do something more challenging before parachuting to the ground. Now skysurfing is a major extreme sport.

SKYSURFERS have to be very fit. They combine surfing, acrobatics, skydiving, and snowboarding in their extreme sport.

I think I'll just rest on this cloud for a bit.

Skysurfers can "surf" the air because of the wind **resistance**. As the wind hits their boards, skysurfers ride air currents like waves. But this is risky. You need to be an expert skydiver before you even think about trying to surf in the sky.

THESE PHOTOGRAPHS were taken by a free-falling cameraflyer. That's a skydiver with a camera strapped to his or her head!

Extreme Endurance

You're running in a marathon. Your legs feel like lead. They burn with every step you take.

But you are determined to make it to the finish line. You must keep going . . .

Some athletes take pain and **endurance** to extreme levels. They push themselves to a point that would kill most people. And they do it again and again— sometimes to win and sometimes just for the thrill of it.

How Low Can You Go?

Free divers hold their breath
and dive as deeply as they can.
Sound easy? It's not! About 50
free divers die every year due to
the body's reaction to **apnea**—not
breathing. So why is this sport so
popular? Probably because it is an incredible
test of what the human body can endure.

YORGOS HAGGI STATTI dived feet first, not head first.

Before diving, the athlete breathes very
deeply to saturate his or her body with oxygen.
Then the diver slows his or her heart rate to
a near-death pace so that the body will need
less oxygen. After one final big breath, the
diver descends into the water.

Divers who come up too quickly can black out.
Even if they get quick medical help, some of
them may not live to dive again.

FREE DIVING has other dangers. During one competition, a diver was taken away by a shark!

Fries with that?

The First Great Free Diver

For centuries, people have dived in deep water for sponges and pearls. But Yorgos Haggi Statti is the man who really started free diving. In 1911, he was on board a ship that lost its anchor. Although Statti suffered from asthma, he offered to dive down to find the anchor and pass a rope through it. No one believed he could do it. After three tries, Statti dived 77.5 meters (254 ft.) and found the anchor.

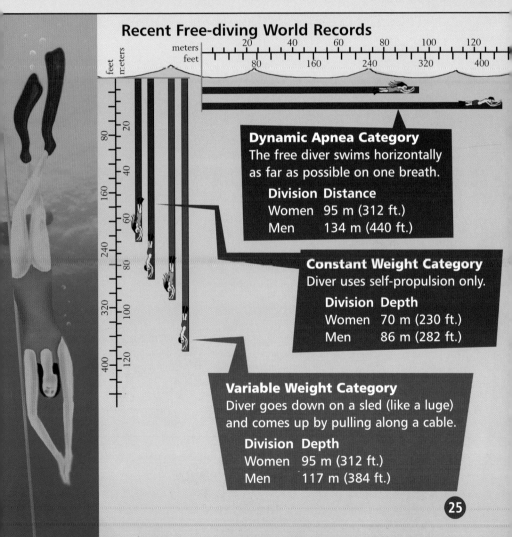

Recent Free-diving World Records

Dynamic Apnea Category
The free diver swims horizontally as far as possible on one breath.

Division	Distance
Women	95 m (312 ft.)
Men	134 m (440 ft.)

Constant Weight Category
Diver uses self-propulsion only.

Division	Depth
Women	70 m (230 ft.)
Men	86 m (282 ft.)

Variable Weight Category
Diver goes down on a sled (like a luge) and comes up by pulling along a cable.

Division	Depth
Women	95 m (312 ft.)
Men	117 m (384 ft.)

Rock Stars

You are halfway up the rock face. It's sharp and steep. Your arms and legs ache. There's only one way to go—up!

You need strong arms, determination, common sense, and great endurance to be a rock climber. It's a slow, painstaking climb up the side of a cliff. Teamwork and trust are also very important to rock climbers. The first climber up the cliff fixes pegs into cracks in the rocks. Then he or she attaches a rope to metal safety devices called **carabiners** (ka-rah-BEE-nerz). The last climber climbs up the rope and removes the carabiners. Slowly, the climbers edge their way up the cliff.

THE FIRST CLIMBER up the cliff plans the route. He or she looks for small cracks in the cliff where fingers can grip.

Q: Why did the man drive over the cliff?
A: *He wanted to test his air brakes.*

Different Levels of Rock Climbing

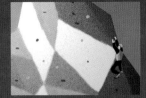
Sport climbing

Bouldering

Big wall

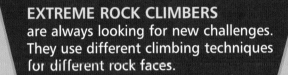

EXTREME ROCK CLIMBERS are always looking for new challenges. They use different climbing techniques for different rock faces.

I wish I hadn't bitten my nails.

CLIMBERS without any safety equipment are "soloing." It is the most dangerous and foolish form of climbing.

Bored? Try-athlon!

There's a race for people who want to push themselves to the absolute limit—it's the triathlon. Competitors in this endurance race have to swim, cycle, and run—with no breaks between events. Most people would have a difficult time trying to complete even one part of this race!

Triathlons are held all over the world, but they may vary in length. The triathlon became an Olympic sport in 2000 at the Olympic Games in Sydney, Australia. The Olympic triathlon consists of a 1.5-kilometer (just under 1-mile) swim, a 40-kilometer (25-mile) bike ride, and a 10-kilometer (6-mile) run. It's hard just to finish a triathlon. To win one is extraordinary!

But then, I'm an extraordinary person!

OFF AND RACING!
Thrashing it out in the swimming event.

NEARING the finish line. Water anyone?

Big

The Ironman Triathlon in Hawaii covers the longest distances of the one-day triathlons. About 1,500 competitors from about 50 countries swim 4 kilometers (about 2½ miles), bike 180 kilometers (112 miles), and run 42 kilometers (about 26 miles). Believe it or not, people have completed this challenging race in less than 8½ hours!

Bigger

In Monterrey, Mexico, in 1988, athletes competed in a triathlon that was 20 times as long as the Ironman Triathlon. The winner of this double deca-triathlon completed the race in about 438 hours—just over 18 days!

EVENT NUMBER TWO. Cyclists hitch a ride in the leader's slipstream.

How does he do it?

Live life to the limit!

FACT FILE

Ahh!

Who said that?

Slovenian daredevil Davo Karnicar climbed to the top of Mount Everest, the world's tallest mountain. Then, he skied back down.

The longest free fall was 25,821 meters (84,715 ft.). The free faller hit 1,006 kilometers per hour (625 mph)—just faster than the speed of sound.

Daniel Goodwin climbed 443 meters (1,454 ft.) up the outside of Chicago's Sears Tower. All he used for safety were suction cups and metal clips.

Hang on to your hat on the Steel Dragon roller coaster in Japan! It hurls riders around its 2,479 meters (8,133 ft.) of track and down its 76-meter (249-ft.) drops—at 148 kilometers per hour (92 mph).

In 1999, professional stuntman Gary Rothwell skied behind his motorcycle wearing boots with metal soles. His cruising speed was 241 kilometers per hour (150 mph).

What's that burni smell?

GLOSSARY

adrenaline a substance produced by the body that acts as a drug to increase heartbeat, reaction speed, and so on

apnea not breathing

avalanches large masses of snow or ice that break away from a mountain and slide down, growing in speed and bulk as they descend

carabiners metal safety devices used in rock climbing

claustrophobic afraid of being in small, confined places

endurance the power to cope with continuous hardship, stress, or strain

hormone a chemical produced by a gland in the body and carried in the blood

resistance the opposition that one thing or force puts against another

spelunking exploring and studying caves

stalactites shapes, formed over time by mineral deposits, that hang from the roof of caves like icicles

stalagmites similar to stalactites except they are found on the floors of caves and grow upwards

INDEX